# THE VITAL ILLUSION

WELLEK LIBRARY LECTURES

# EDITORIAL NOTE

The Wellek Library Lectures in Critical Theory are given annually at the University of California, Irvine, under the auspices of the Critical Theory Institute. The following lectures were given in May 1999.

*The Critical Theory Institute*

*John Carlos Rowe, Director*

# THE VITAL ILLUSION

Jean Baudrillard

*Edited by Julia Witwer*

Columbia University Press  New York

Columbia University Press
Publishers Since 1893
New York   Chichester, West Sussex
Copyright © 2000 Columbia University Press

Library of Congress Cataloging-in-Publication Data
Baudrillard, Jean.
The vital illusion / Jean Baudrillard ;
edited by Julia Witwer.
p. cm – (Wellek Library lectures)
Includes index.
ISBN 0–231–12100–8
1. Reality. 2. Virtual reality. 3. Cloning.
I. Witwer, Julia. II. Title.
III. Wellek Library lectures at the
University of California Irving.
BD331 .B287 2000
194–dc21          00–034567

Casebound editions of Columbia University Press books
are printed on permanent and durable acid-free paper.
Printed in the United States of America
*Designed by Audrey Smith*

c 10 9 8 7 6 5 4 3 2 1

# CONTENTS

# THE VITAL ILLUSION

# 1

THE FINAL SOLUTION:
CLONING BEYOND
THE HUMAN
AND INHUMAN

The question concerning cloning is the question of immortality. We all want immortality. It is our ultimate fantasy, a fantasy that is also at work in all of our modern sciences and technologies—at work, for example, in the deep freeze of cryonic suspension and in cloning in all its manifestations.

The most notorious example of cryonic suspension is—naturally—Walt Disney, but he, at least, being destined for resurrection, is said to have been frozen whole, in his "integrity." There are more anomalous situations today. Nowadays, in Phoenix, Arizona (the predestined site for Resurrection), only the heads are frozen, because it's from the cells of the brain—regarded as the nucleus of individual being—that researchers hope to reconstitute the deceased in their bodily wholeness. (One can't help but wonder why they don't, in that case, simply preserve a single cell or a DNA molecule.)

To complement these heads without bodies: On the other side of the Atlantic Ocean, headless frogs and mice are being cloned in private laboratories, in preparation for the cloning of headless human bodies that will serve as reservoirs for organ donation. Why bodies without heads? As the head is considered the site of consciousness, it is thought that bodies *with heads* would pose ethical and psychological problems. Better simply to manufacture acephalic creatures whose organs could be freely harvested, because such creatures would not compete with—or invoke too closely—the original human beings.

These, then, are the experimental and artificial forms of cloning—not including Dolly, of course, and the rest of her kind. But spontaneous cloning, and in fact spontaneous immortality, can also be found in nature, at the heart of our cells.

Ordinarily, a cell is destined to divide a certain number of times and then to die. If, in the course of its division, something happens to perturb this process—for example, an alteration in the gene that prevents tumors or in the mechanisms governing cellular apoptosis—then the cell becomes cancerous. It *forgets to die*; it forgets *how* to die. It goes on to clone itself again and again, making thousands of identical copies of itself, thus forming a tumor. Normally the subject dies as a result, and the cancerous cells die with him or her. But in the case of Henrietta Lacks, the tumor cells sampled from her body were cultured in a laboratory and will continue to proliferate endlessly. They constitute so remarkable and virulent a specimen that they have been circulated throughout the world and even sent into space, on board the U.S. satellite Discoverer 17. So it is that the disseminated body of Henrietta Lacks, cloned at the molecular level, makes its immortal rounds.

—·—

There is something occulted inside us: our death. But something else is hidden there, lying in wait for us within each of our cells: the forgetting of death. In our cells our immortality lies in wait for us. It's common to speak of the struggle of life against death, but there is an inverse peril. And we must struggle against the possibility that we will not die. At the slightest hesitation in the fight for death—a fight for division, for sex, for alterity, and so for death—living beings become once again indivisible, identical to one another—and immortal.

Contrary to everything that seems obvious and "natural," nature's first creatures were immortal. It was only by obtaining the power to die, by dint of constant struggle, that we became the living beings we are today. Blindly we dream of overcoming death through immortality, when all the time immortality is the most horrific of possible fates. Encoded in the earliest life of our cells, this fate is now reappearing on our horizons, so to speak, with the advent of cloning. (The death drive, according to Freud, is precisely this nostalgia for a state before the appearance of individuality and sexual differentiation, a state in which we lived before we became mortal and distinct from one another. Absolute death is not the end of the individual human being; rather, it is a regression toward a state of minimal differentiation among living beings, of a pure repetition of identical beings.)

The evolution of the biosphere is what drives immortal beings to become mortal ones. They move, little by little, from the absolute continuity found in the subdivision of the same–in bacteria–toward the possibility of birth and death. Next, the egg becomes fertilized by a sperm and specialized sex cells make their appearance. The resulting entity is no longer a copy of either one of the pair that engendered it; rather, it is a new and singular combination. There is a shift from pure and simple reproduction to procreation: the first two will die for the first time, and the *third* for the first time will be born. We reach the stage of beings that are sexed, differentiated, and mortal. The earlier order of the virus–of immortal beings–is perpetuated, but henceforward this world of deathless things is contained inside the world of the mortals. In evolutionary terms, the victory goes to beings that are mortal and distinct from one another: the victory goes to us.

But the game isn't over yet, and reversion is always possible. It can be found not only in the viral revolt of our cells but also in the enormous enterprise we living beings ourselves undertake today: a project to reconstruct a homogeneous and uniformly consistent universe–an artificial continuum this time–that unfolds within a technological and mechanical medium, extending over our vast information network, where we are in the process of building a perfect clone, an identical copy of our world, a virtual artifact that opens up the prospect of endless reproduction.

We are in the process of reactivating this pathological immortality, the immortality of the cancer cell, both at the individual level and at the level of the species as a whole. This is the revenge taken on mortal and sexed beings by immortal and undifferentiated life forms. This is what could be called the final solution.

After the great *revolution* in the evolutionary process—the advent of sex and death—we have the great *involution*: it aims, through cloning and many other techniques, to liberate us from sex and death. Where once living creatures strove, over millions of years, to pull themselves free of this kind of incest and primitive entropy, we are now, through scientific advances themselves, in the process of recreating precisely these conditions. We are actively working at the "dis-information" of our species through the nullification of differences.

Here we must pose the question of the destination of the

scientific project. We must consider the possibility that the very "progress" of science in fact does not follow a line, but a curve—a twisted or hairpin curve that turns back toward total involution. And we must ask if this final solution toward which we unconsciously work is not the secret destination of nature, as well as of all our efforts. This throws a fairly harsh light on everything we still, today, persist in regarding as a positive evolution, as a *step forward*.

———

The sexual revolution—the real one, the *only* one—is the advent of sexuality in the evolution of living things, of a duality that puts an end to perpetual indivision and successive iterations of the same. In this, the sexual revolution is also the revolution of death. It is the revolution of death, as opposed to the infinite survival of the same. The inverse movement we are describing here is an *involutionary* movement of the species, a retreat from the revolution of sex and death, a massive revisionist movement in the evolution of living things.

From this point of view, "sexual liberation" is thoroughly

ambivalent. Though sexual liberation seems at first to be in keeping with the sexual revolution of which it is the final, positive, and definitive moment, it seems, upon further analysis, to have ambiguous repercussions. In the end these repercussions may be completely opposed to the goals of the sexual revolution itself.

The first phase of sexual liberation involves the dissociation of sexual activity from procreation through the pill and other contraceptive devices—a transformation with enormous consequences. The second phase, which we are beginning to enter now, is the dissociation of reproduction from sex. First, sex was liberated from reproduction; today it is reproduction that is liberated from sex, through asexual, biotechnological modes of reproduction such as artificial insemination or full body cloning. This is also a liberation, though antithetical to the first. We've been sexually liberated, and now we will find ourselves liberated from sex— that is, virtually relieved of the sexual function. Among the clones (and among human beings soon enough), sex, as a result of this automatic means of reproduction, becomes extraneous, a useless function. Thus sexual liberation, the so-called crowning achievement of the evolution of sexed forms of life, marks, in its final consequences, the end of the sexual revolution. It is the same ambiguity that troubles science. The calculated benefits both of sexual liberation and of the scientific revolution are inextricably bound up with with their negative countereffects.

And death? Entwined as it is with sex, it must eventually suffer the same fate. There is, in effect, a liberation from death that parallels liberation from sex. As we have dissociated reproduction from sex, so we try to dissociate life from death. To save and promote life and life only, and to render death an obsolete function one can do without, as, in the case of artificial reproduction, we can do without sex.

So death, as a fatal or symbolic event, must be erased. Death must be included only as virtual reality, as an option or changeable setting in the living being's operating system. This is a reprogramming that proceeds along the lines of the virtualization of sex, the "cybersex" that waits for us in the future, as a sort of ontological "attraction." All these useless functions—sex, thought, death—will be redesigned, redesignated as leisure activities. And human beings, henceforth

useless, might themselves be preserved as a kind of ontological "attraction." This could be another aspect of what
Hegel has called the moving life of what is dead. Death,
once a vital function, could thus become a luxury, a diver-
sion. In future modes of civilization, from which death will
have been eliminated, clones of the future may well pay for
the luxury of dying and become mortal once again in simulation: cyberdeath.⟩ 11-2

A sort of anticipation of cloning can be found in nature
itself, in the phenomenon of twins and twinship (*gemellité*).
We can perceive a kind of cloning in the hallucinatory
redoubling of the same, in the primitive symmetry that
makes the two twins seem to be like two halves of a single
self, of the same individual–and we escape the phantasm
only by way of a break, a rupture of the symmetry. But perhaps we have never properly escaped our double; and
cloning, then, may simply be reviving this hallucination of
the same, of the twin from whom we have never quite been
separated. At the same time we may see in cloning the resur-
gence of our fascination with an archaic form of incest with
the original twin, and the grave psychotic consequences of

such a primitive fantasy (Cronenberg's film *Dead Ringers* is a dramatic illustration of this).

Most of the time this twinship remains obscure and symbolic, but whenever it materializes, it illuminates the mystery of the symbolic separation, of the invisible division found at the heart of each of us. (Indeed, there are some who claim to have discovered its biological trace.) From this internal division surely comes the sacred, or rather the accursed character of twinship in every culture. In our culture, however, we also see the other side of this accursedness—the endless resentment and remorse associated with individuation. It is effectively only through this original separation, this "ontological" cleavage from the twin, that the individual being first appears and, with it, the possibility of alterity and of a dual relation. And so we are individuated, and proud of it; but somewhere inside, in an unconscious still deeper than the psychological unconscious, we never overcome, we never fully accept this separation and this individuation.

Is there not a terror of and a nostalgia for this double, and, to go further, for the whole multiplicity of *semblables* from whom we have divided ourselves in the course of evolution? Do we not, after all, deeply regret our individuation?

In effect, we have here a double repentance. Not only do we repent of the emancipation of the individual from the species but, more profoundly still, we repent of having become sexed forms of life, of our evolution from the inorganic to the living world. That is how it goes. Any given liberation, emancipation, or individuation is also experienced as anomie and as betrayal, in fact as the source of endless neurosis, a neurosis that becomes increasingly serious as one moves further away from the nostalgic point of origin. Liberty is hard to take. Life itself, finally, may be hard to take, as a rupturing of the inorganic chain of matter. In a way it is the revenge of the species, the revenge of the immortal forms of life that we thought we had overcome.

In cloning–this collective fantasy of a return to a non-individuated existence and a destiny of undifferentiated life, this temptation to return to an indifferent immortality–we see the very form of a repentance of the living toward the unliving. This repentance arises from the depths of a past time; we pine for a state that is long gone but that will be possible again by virtue of our technologies, becoming eventually an object of our fascination, our nostalgia, and our desire.

This may well be the story of a deliberate project to put an end to the genetic game of difference, to stop the divagations of the living. Aren't we actually sick of sex, of difference, of emancipation, of culture? The world of individuals and social relations itself offers striking examples of this exhaustion—or resistance—or nostalgic attachment to some prior state of being. In any case, we are dealing with a kind of revisionism, a crucial revision of the whole process of evolution and especially that of the human race—a species unable to brave its own diversity, its own complexity, its own radical difference, its own alterity.

But perhaps we may see this as a kind of adventure, a heroic test: to take the artificialization of living beings as far as possible in order to see, finally, what part of human nature survives the great ordeal. If we discover that not everything can be cloned, simulated, programmed, genetically and neurologically managed, then whatever survives

could truly be called "human": some inalienable and inde-
structible human quality could finally be identified. Of
course, there is always the risk, in this experimental adventure, that nothing will pass the test—that the human will be
permanently eradicated.

Such was the lesson of Biosphere 2, the artificial synthesis of all the planet's systems, the ideal copy of the human
race and its environment. Biosphere 2 reveals in miniature
the fact that the human race and the entire planet are
already becoming their own virtual reality, that underneath
its vast geodesic dome of information, the planet has
already embarked on an experimental path from which
there is no return. From this moment on it is possible to ask
if we are still dealing with human beings. Is a species that
succeeds in synthesizing its own immortality, and that seeks
to transform itself into pure information, still particularly a
human species?

Humankind does not discriminate; it willingly becomes
its own guinea pig under the same terms as the rest of the
world, animate and inanimate. Humankind blithely plays
with its own future as a species in the same way that it

plays with the future of all other creatures. In its blind quest to possess greater knowledge, humankind programs its own destruction with the same casual ferocity that it applies to the destruction of everything else. You could hardly accuse humanity of egocentrism. Humanity sacrifices itself as a whole species to an unknown experimental fate—unknown before this, in any case, to other species, who have never known any fate but a natural one. And while this natural destiny would seem related to something like an instinct for self-preservation, the new experimental destiny to which the human race devotes itself sweeps away all instinct for self-preservation. The disappearance of this concept from the fields of research indicates that, behind the ecological obsession with protection and conservation—which has much more to do with nostalgia and remorse—an entirely different inclination has taken over: the inclination to sacrifice the entire species to limitless experimentation.

And so a double and contradictory movement: Humankind, alone among all living things, tries to build itself a deathless alter ego and at the same time to perfect natural

selection through artificial selection—an act that confers
on the human being an absolute privilege. Yet at the same
time and precisely through this action, humankind puts an
end to natural selection, a process that implies, according
to the laws of evolution, the death of any given species—
including its own. By ending natural selection, humankind
contravenes symbolic law, and in so doing effectively risks
its own disappearance. Not, this time, because of natural
law, but by way of its detour. In their arrogant plan to bring
evolution to an end, human beings set in motion the involution of their own kind, which is in the process of losing
its specificity, its very immunity. For the death rate of artificial species is even more rapid than that of natural
species. By taking an artificial course, our species may be
running all the more quickly into its own decline. ⌋

All this derives from a strange fact: apparently, the
human race cannot bear itself, cannot bear to be reconciled
to itself. Paralleling the violence it wreaks on other living
things, there is a violence peculiar to humankind, wreaked
by itself on itself. It is as if, through this self-inflicted violence, humanity wants to make itself ready from now on to

be the survivor of some great impending catastrophe. As if, all the while being proud and convinced of its superiority, humankind nevertheless resents the evolutionary process that has elevated it to this privileged position and pushed it, in some fashion, beyond its natural limits as a species.

The same configuration appears in Canetti's description of our exit from history. In experimentation we find a similar movement, but this time it is a passage out of the human per se, a passage even more fatal, a movement toward the point beyond which we can recognize neither human nor inhuman. Much like the point, in Canetti, beyond which the words "truth" and "falsehood" no longer have any meaning. Indeed, to push Canetti's analysis further, the stakes are no longer only that "history" is slipping into the "posthistorical," but that the human race is slipping into the void.

Have we come, via an unexpected detour, to the same point at which animal species, when they reach a critical saturation point, automatically switch over to a kind of collective suicide?

The inhumanity of this undertaking is legible in the abolition of all that is "human, all too human" in us: our desires, our failings, our neuroses, our dreams, our handicaps, our viruses, our frenzies, our unconscious, and even our sexuality. Prescriptions are being placed on all the specific qualities that make us unique living beings. The specter that haunts genetic manipulation is the genetic ideal, a perfect model obtained through the elimination of all negative traits. In the experimental prototype Biosphere 2, for example, we find no viruses, no germs, no scorpions . . . and no sexual reproduction. Everything in Biosphere 2 has been purified, immunized–immortalized–through transparency, disincarnation, and prophylactic disinfection.

Life becomes sheer survival when it is reduced to the lowest common denominator, to the genome, the genetic inheritance–where it is the perpetual movement of the DNA codes that drives life, and where the distinctive marks of the human fade before the metonymic eternity of cells. The worst of it is that living beings engendered by their own genetic formulae doubtless will not survive this process of reduction. That which lives and survives by the codes will die by them.

The limits of the human and the inhuman are in the

process of being worn away—but the human does not give way to the superhuman, as Nietzsche had dreamed, with his transvaluation of values. Rather, it gives way to the subhuman, to something not beyond but underneath the human, to an erasure of those symbolic marks that make up the species. A fact that proves that Nietzsche was right after all when he said the human race, left to its own devices, is capable only of redoubling its efforts, of re-doubling itself—or of destroying itself.

———

Traditional humanism, that of the Enlightenment, was based on the qualities of man, on his natural gifts and virtues—on his essence, which went hand-in-hand with his right to liberty and the exercise of that liberty. Contemporary humanism, in its expanded version, is affiliated more and more with the preservation of the individual and of humankind as a genetically defined entity. When we look behind the Rights of Man, we no longer find a moral or sovereign being, but instead the prerogatives of an endangered species. Then these rights become problematic, for they pose the question of the rights of other species, or of children, or of nature itself–in contrast to which the human species has to define itself.

But is there even a *genetic* definition of the human? And if it does exist, does a species have rights to its own genome and to its own eventual genetic transformation? We share 98 percent of our genes with apes and fully 90 percent of them with mice. Based on this common inheritance, what rights shall revert to the apes and the mice? Furthermore, it appears that some 90 percent of the genes making up our genome serve no purpose at all. What right do these genes have to exist? This is a critical question: if we describe them as useless, we arrogate to ourselves the right to destroy them.

The same thing goes for any given aspect of humanity itself: once the human is no longer defined in terms of transcendence and liberty, but in terms of functions and of biological equilibrium, the definition of the human itself begins to fade, along with that of humanism. Occidental humanism was already challenged by the irruption of other cultures as early as the sixteenth century. Now the assault is not only against a particular culture but against the whole species: *anthropological* deregulation, along with the deregulation of all the moral, juridical, and symbolic codes that founded humanism. Is it possible to speak of the soul, or the conscience, or even of the unconscious from the point of view of the automatons, the chimeras, and the clones that will supersede the human race? Both the individual and the species's capital are jeopardized by the erosion of the limits of the human, by the slide, not just into the inhuman but into something that is neither human nor inhuman: namely, the genetic simulation of life.

The mutual interplay between human and inhuman–the balance between them–has been disrupted. Certainly the eventual disappearance of the human is very serious, but the loss of the inhuman is no less serious. The specificity of the inhuman–and of that *within* the human being that is, so to speak, inhuman–is being threatened by the hegemony of the human, according to its definition as thoroughly modern, thoroughly rational, and thoroughly Western in character. The impulse to annex nature, animals, other races and cultures–to put them universally under jurisdiction–is in effect everywhere. Everything is assigned a place within an evolutionist and hegemonic anthropology, in a veritable triumph of uniform thought, of a monothought (*une pensée unique*) of the human—as defined by the West, under the sign of the universal and of democracy. The Rights of Man today are the vector of this anthropic, anthropocratic thought, behind which the human and the inhuman proliferate—in apparent contradiction but in actual complicity with one another. And so we now experience both the "improvement" of human rights and the recrudescence of their violation.

Non-Occidental cultures do not discriminate between the human and the inhuman. *We* invented the distinction, and *we* are in the process of erasing it. Not by crossing the line and reconciling the two; rather, the erasure operates in absentia, through technological undifferentiation.

Again: the final solution, the vertigo of a final solution.

It might be argued that whatever the genetic destination of the clone may be, it will never be exactly the same as the original. (Well, of course not, as the clone will have had an Original, which cannot be said of the original itself.) But the main argument is that there is nothing to fear from bio-genetically engineered cloning, because whatever happens, culture will continue to differentiate us. Salvation lies in our acquirements: culture alone will preserve us from the hell of the Same.

In fact, exactly the reverse is true. It is culture that clones us, and mental cloning anticipates any biological cloning. It is the matrix of acquired traits that, today, clones us cultur-ally under the sign of monothought—and it is all the innate differences that are annulled, inexorably, by ideas, by ways of life, by the cultural context. Through school systems, media, culture, and mass information, singular beings become identical copies of one another. It is this kind of cloning—social cloning, the industrial reproduction of things and people—that makes possible the biological con-ception of the genome and of genetic cloning, which only further sanctions the cloning of human conduct and human cognition.

All this radically alters the ethical questions surrounding the prescriptive limits on cloning and the rights of the indi-vidual facing scientific and technological experimentation–in short, everything that is currently being discussed by the ethics boards and the committees for collective moral thought. Yet beyond their political, ideological, and commercial purposes, the speculations of the committees are useless, since it is the culture of difference itself, our humanist ethos *itself*, that works most efficiently in the direction of undifferentiation, of human Xerox copies, and of mono-thought. This new regime has at least some positive aspect, however, insofar as it offers us the chance to call into question the basic elements of millenarian morality.

This matter of the clones, in fact, could call a number of things into question–and that is the irony of the situation. The clone, after all, could also appear as a grotesque parody of the original. It is not hard to imagine a whole range of potential problems and new conflicts issuing from cloning that would turn oedipal psychology upside down. Consider, for instance, a clone of the future overthrowing his father, not in order to sleep with his mother–which would be impossible, anyway, since she is nothing but a matrix of cells, and besides, the "father" could very well be a woman– but in order to secure his status as the Original. Or imagine, instead, the disenfranchised original working his revenge on his clone . . . all sorts of conflicts that would no longer center on the child and his or her parents but on the original and its double. It is possible to imagine entirely new functions for clones, quite different from those assigned them today, which all hinge on the perpetuation of life. For instance, they could function as instruments for the satisfaction of the death instinct—as recipients of a death wish. Kill your clone, destroy yourself with no risk of actually dying: vicarious suicide.

But our moralists and our biologists are not yet at this point; they have not yet discovered the operation of the death drive as a fundamental part of the human individual and of the human race. For just as there is a drive for immortality, to which techniques such as cloning respond, so there is a death drive. As we have seen, these drives are in play simultaneously, and it is possible that one is nothing but a variant of the other, nothing but its detour.

The silver lining of this fatal enterprise is that it reveals to us something that radical philosophies already know: there is no morality to oppose to this immoral desire, this technological desire for immortality. There are no laws of nature and no moral law that would be their manifestation. The notion of such a law springs from an idealized vision of the world, one that is perpetuated, I would add, by science itself. There are no natural rights of the individual, or of the species, from the point of view of an ideal definition. Thus there is no interdiction that could be founded on a division between good and evil.

There is, however, a different division. The stakes are not moral but symbolic. There are rules to the game of living, whose forms are secret, whose finality is inscrutable. Life "means" nothing, not even human life; if it is precious, it's not as a value but as a form, a form that exceeds all individual and collective value. Today, life is preserved insofar as it has value, that is, insofar as it has exchange value. But if life is precious, it is because it has no exchange value—because exchanging it for some ultimate value is impossible. The world is that which cannot be traded as currency for any other world, above all for a virtual world. The human is that which cannot be traded as currency for any given artificial species, such as clones, even if the clones perform better, are a "better value." A form—and life is a form—can only be exchanged with another form, never traded for an equivalent. There is a change from one form to another, but there is no way to exchange a form for a general equivalent.

In this respect, the forms—the species, or life itself—obey no moral law but are vectors of a vital illusion. Thus it makes no sense to oppose the immortality of the Same, of repetition, of the clone, of the virus, with a morality of values and differences; it is necessary to oppose *immortality* with the superior *immorality* of forms. And of thought, also—for thought is another thing that cannot be exchanged, either for some objective truth (as in science) or for an artificial double, such as artificial intelligence. Thought is singular, and in its singularity thought may be able to protect us.

Thus, a double movement: first the reign of the immortals, then the mortal and sexed beings overtaking the immortals; Today, however, the immortals are silently avenging themselves through the processes of cloning, through interminable reduplication, through the obliteration of sex and death.

But this game is not yet over. We can count on fierce

resistance from the mortal creatures that we are, a resistance that springs out of the depths of the species, its vital exigency, its refusal of any final solution. This refusal is not a matter of human rights; it is a matter of life and death.

# 2

THE MILLENNIUM, OR
THE SUSPENSE OF THE
YEAR 2000

How can we jump over our shadows when we no longer have any? How can we pass out of the old century (not to speak of the millennium) if we do not make up our minds to put an end to it, engaged as we are in an indefinite work of mourning for all the incidents, ideologies, and violence that have marked it? The—more or less hypocritical—commemorations and recantations give the impression that we are trying to run the events of the century back through the filter of memory, not in order to find a meaning for them—they have clearly lost that meaning somewhere along the way—but in order to whitewash them, or to launder them. Cleansing is the prime activity of this fin de siècle—the laundering of a dirty history, of dirty money, of corrupt consciousnesses, of the polluted planet—the cleansing of memory being indissolubly linked to the (hygienic) cleansing of the environment or to the (racial and ethnic) cleansing of populations. We are turning away from history "in progress," with none of the problems it poses having been resolved, and plunging into a regressive history, in the nostalgic hope of making something politically correct out of it. And in this retrospective, necrospective obsession, we are losing any chance of things coming to their term. This is why I advanced the idea that the Year 2000 would not take place—quite simply, because the history of this century had already come to an end, because we are remaking it interminably and because, therefore, metaphorically speaking, we shall never pass on, into the future.

Our millenarianism—for we have reached, all the same, a millenarian deadline—is a millenarianism with no tomorrow. Whereas the coming of the Year 1000, even though it was experienced with dread, was a prelude to *parousia* and to the advent of the Kingdom of God, and hence the prelude to an infinite promise, our own deadline remains a closed, involuted one. All we have left of the millenarian dateline is the countdown to it. A perfect symbol for the century—which could do nothing more than count the seconds separating it from its end—is the digital clock on the Beaubourg Center in Paris that showed the countdown in millions of seconds. It illustrates the reversal of our modern relation to time. Time is no longer counted progressively, by addition, starting from an origin—but by subtraction, starting from the end. This is what happens with rocket launches and time bombs. And that end is no longer the symbolic endpoint of a history but the mark of a zero sum, of a potential exhaustion. Time is viewed from a perspective of entropy—the exhausting of all possibilities—the perspective of a counting down ... to infinity. We no longer possess a forward-looking, historical, or providential vision, which was the vision of a world of progress or production. The final illusion of history, the final utopia of time no longer exists, since it is already registered there as something potentially accounted for, calculated in digital time, just as the finalities of the human cease to exist at the point where they come to be registered in a genetic capital and are looked at solely from the biological perspective of the exploitation of the genome. When you count the seconds separating you from the end, it means that everything is already at an end, that moreover we are already beyond the end.

By the way: something happened to this digital clock. It

was removed from the front of the Beaubourg, relegated to a storehouse at the Parc de la Villette without anyone knowing about it. For a long time it was there ticking in the dark—a very heavy symbol of the destiny of Time at the end of the twentieth century. Then it was displaced again to the Place de la Bastille (the story of the inventor and the EDF: time doesn't work anymore). This is a truly illuminating emblem of Y2K's failure to take place. Even the sign of it was removed in anticipation. It seems that no right place is to be found for the end.

Was it for fear of this deadline? Growing anxiety about this deadline? Or did it mean, as we said, that this end had already occurred, secretly, furtively—perhaps at the very beginning of the countdown?—and that it now lay behind us? And then the registration of it would be useless. The same thing goes for the Apocalypse. The real event of the Apocalypse is behind us, among us, and we are instead confronted with the virtual reality of the Apocalypse, with the posthumous comedy of the Apocalypse. Maybe it was already the same with the first millennium, with the Apocalypse of Y1K. "The writers of the Apocalypse send letter after letter to one another, instead of questioning the Antichrist himself." Then, even they were already dealing with the virtual reality of the Apocalypse.

In the countdown, the time remaining is already past, and the maximal utopia of life gives way to the minimal utopia of survival. We are experiencing time and history in a kind of deep coma. This is the hysteresis of the millennium, which expresses itself in interminable crisis. It is no longer the future that lies before us, but an anorectic dimension–the impossibility of anything's being over and, at the same time, the impossibility of seeing beyond the present. Prediction, the memory of the future, diminishes in exact proportion to the memory of the past. When there is overall transparence, when everything can be seen, nothing can be *foreseen* anymore.

—·—

What is there beyond the end? Beyond the end extends virtual reality, the horizon of a programmed reality in which all our functions–memory, emotions, sexuality, intelligence–become progressively useless. Beyond the end, in the era of the transpolitical, the transsexual, the transaesthetic, all our desiring machines become little spectacle machines, then quite simply bachelor machines, before trailing off into the countdown of the species. The countdown is the code of the automatic disappearance of the world, and all our little charitable machines, by way of which we anticipate that disappearance–the Telethons, Sidathons, and all kinds of Thanathons–are merely the promotional sales events for the misery of this fin de siècle.

But–and this is even more paradoxical–what are we to do when nothing really comes to an end anymore, that is to say, when nothing ever really takes place, since everything is already calculated, audited, and realized in advance (the simulacrum preceding the real, information preceding the event, etc.)? Our problem is no longer: What are we to make of real events, of real violence? Rather, it is: What are we to make of events that do not take place? Not: What are we to do after the orgy? But: What are we to do when the orgy no longer takes place–the orgy of history, the orgy of revolution and liberation, the orgy of modernity? Little by little, as the hands of the clock move around (though, sadly, digital clocks no longer even have hands), we tell ourselves that, taking everything into account–taking everything into a "count-down"–modernity has never happened. There has never really been any modernity, never any real progress, never any assured liberation. The linear tension of modernity and progress has been broken, the thread of history has become tangled: the last great "historic" event–the fall of the Berlin Wall–signified something closer to an enormous repentance on the part of history. Instead of seeking fresh perspectives, history appears rather to be splintering into scattered fragments, and phases of events and conflicts we had thought long gone are being reactivated.

All that we believed over and done, left behind by the inexorable march of universal progress, is not dead at all; it seems to be returning to strike at the heart of our ultra-sophisticated, ultravulnerable systems. It's a bit like the last scene of *Jurassic Park*, in which the modern (artificially cloned) dinosaurs burst into the museum and wreak havoc on their fossilized ancestors preserved there, before being destroyed in their turn. Today we are caught as a species in a similar impasse, trapped between our fossils and our clones.

So, the countdown extends in both directions: not only

does it put an end to time in the future but it also exhausts itself in the obsessional revival of the events of the past. A reversed recapitulation, which is the opposite of a living memory–it is fanatical *memorization*, a fascination with commemorations, rehabilitations, cultural museification, the listing of sites of memory, the extolling of heritage. In fact this obsession with reliving and reviving everything, this obsessional neurosis, this forcing of memory is equivalent to a vanishing of memory–a vanishing of actual history, a vanishing of the event in the information space. This amounts to making the past itself into a clone, an artificial double, and freezing it in a sham exactitude that will never actually do it justice. But it is because we have nothing else, now, but objects in which not to believe, nothing but fossilized hopes, that we are forced to go down this road: to elevate everything to the status of a museum piece, an item of heritage. Here again, time reverses: instead of things first passing through history before becoming part of the heritage, they now pass directly into the heritage. Instead of first existing, works of art now go straight into the museum. Instead of being born and dying, beings are "born" as virtual fossils. Collective neurosis. As a result, the ozone layer that was protecting memory becomes frayed; the hole through which memories and time are leaking out into space expands, prefiguring the great migration of the void to the periphery.

———

Closing down, closing down! It's the end-of-the-century sale. Everything must go! Modernity is over (without ever having happened), the orgy is over, the party is over–the sales are starting. It's the great end-of-the-century sale. But the sales don't come after the festive seasons any longer; nowadays the sales start first, they last the whole year long, even the festivals themselves are on sale everywhere.... The stocks have to be used up, time-capital has to be used up, life-capital has to be used up. Everywhere, we have the countdown; what we are living through in this symbolic end of the old millennium is a sort of fatal prescription, whether it be that of the planet's resources or of AIDS, which has become the collective symptom of the prescribed term of death. It is all these things that hang over us in the shadow of the Year 2000, together with the delicious, yet terrifying enjoyment of the lag time left to us. But, ultimately, perhaps the Year 2000 will not have taken place? Perhaps, on the occasion of the Year 2000, we are to be granted a general amnesty?

The concept of countdown evokes once again Arthur C. Clarke's "The Nine Billion Names of God." A community of Tibetan monks has been engaged from time immemorial in listing and copying out the names of God, of which there are nine billion. At the end of this, the world will end. So runs the prophecy. But the monks are tired and, in order to hasten the work, they call in the experts at IBM, who come along with their computers and finish the job in a month. It is as if the operation of the virtual dimension were to bring the history of the world to an end in an instant. Unfortunately, this also means the disappearance of the world in real time, for the prophecy of the end of the world associated with this countdown of the names of God is fulfilled. As they go back down into the valley, the technicians, who did not actually believe the prophecy, see the stars vanishing from the firmament, one by one.

This parable depicts our modern situation well: we have called in the IBM technicians and they have launched the code of the world's automatic disappearance. As a result of the intervention of all the digital, computing, and virtual-reality technologies, we are already beyond reality; things have already passed beyond their own ends. They cannot, therefore, come to an end any longer, and they sink into the interminable (interminable history, interminable politics, interminable crisis).

And, in effect, we persevere, on the pretext of an increasingly sophisticated technology, in the endless deconstruction of a world and of a history unable to transcend and complete itself. Everything is free to go on infinitely. We no longer have the means to end processes. They unfold without us now, beyond reality, so to speak, in an endless speculation, an exponential acceleration. But, as a result, they do so in an indifference that is also exponential. What is endless is also desire-less, tension-less, passionless; it is bereft of events. An anorectic history, no longer fueled by real incidents and exhausting itself in the countdown. Exactly the opposite of the end of history, then: *the impossibility of finishing with history*. If history can no longer reach its end, then it is, properly speaking, no longer a history. We have lost history and have also, as a result, lost the end of history. We are laboring under the illusion of the end, under the posthumous illusion of the end. And this is serious, for the end signifies that something has really taken place. Whereas we, at the height of reality—and with information at its peak—no longer know whether anything has taken place or not.

Perhaps the end of history, if we can actually conceive such a thing, is merely ironic? Perhaps it is merely an effect of the ruse of history, which consists in its having concealed the end from us, in its having ended without our noticing it. So that it is merely the end of history that is being fueled, whereas we believe we are continuing to make it. We are still awaiting its end, whereas that end has, in fact, already taken place. History's ruse was to make us believe in its end, when it has, in fact, already started back in the opposite direction.

Whether we speak of the end of history, the end of the political or the end of the social, what we are clearly dealing with is the end of *the scene of the political*, the end of *the scene of the social*, the end of *the scene of history*. In other words, in all these spheres, we are speaking of the advent of a specific era of *obscenity*. Obscenity may be characterized as the endless, unbridled proliferation of the social, of the political, of information, of the economic, of the aesthetic, not to mention the sexual. Obesity is another of the figures of obscenity. As proliferation, as the saturation of a limitless space, obesity may stand as a general metaphor for our systems of information, communication, production, and memory. Obesity and obscenity form the contrapuntal figure for all our systems, which have been seized by something of an Ubuesque distension. All our structures end up swelling like red giants that absorb everything in their expansion. Thus the social sphere, as it expands, absorbs the political sphere entirely. But the political sphere is itself obese and obscene—and yet at the same time it is becoming increasingly transparent. The more it distends, the more it virtually ceases to exist. When everything is political, that is the end of politics as destiny; it is the beginning of politics as culture and the immediate poverty of that cultural politics. It is the same with the economic or the sexual spheres. As it dilates, each structure infiltrates and subsumes the others, before being absorbed in its turn.

Such are the extreme phenomena: those that occur

beyond the end (extreme = *ex terminis*). They indicate that we have passed from growth (*croissance*) to outgrowth (*excroissance*), from movement and change to stasis, *ek*-stasis, and metastasis. They countersign the end, marking it by excess, hypertrophy, proliferation, and chain reaction; they reach critical mass, overstep the critical deadline, through potentiality and exponentiality.

> Ecstasy of the social: the masses. More social than the social.
>
> Ecstasy of the body: obesity. Fatter than fat.
>
> Ecstasy of information: simulation. Truer than true.
>
> Ecstasy of time: real time, instantaneity. More present than the present.
>
> Ecstasy of the real: the hyperreal. More real than the real.
>
> Ecstasy of sex: porn. More sexual than sex.
>
> Ecstasy of violence: terror. More violent than violence. . . .

All this describes, by a kind of potentiation, a raising to the second power, a pushing to the limit, a state of unconditional realization, of total positivity (every negative sign raised to the second power produces a positive), from which all utopia, all death, and all negativity have been expunged. A state of ex-termination, cleansing of the negative, as corollary to all the other actual forms of purification and discrimination. Thus, freedom has been obliterated, liquidated by liberation; truth has been supplanted by verification; the community has been liquidated and absorbed by communication; form gives way to information and performance. Everywhere we see a paradoxical logic: the idea is destroyed by its own realization, by its own excess. And in this way history itself comes to an end, finds itself obliterated by the instantaneity and omnipresence of the event.

This kind of acceleration by inertia, this exponentiality of extreme phenomena, produces a new kind of event: now we encounter strange, altered, random, and chaotic events that Historical Reason no longer recognizes as its own. Even if, by analogy with past events, we think we recognize them, they no longer have the same meaning. The same incidents (wars, ethnic conflicts, nationalisms, the unification of Europe) do not have the same meaning when they arise as part of a history in progress as they do in the context of a history in decline. Now, we find ourselves in a vanishing history, and that is why they appear as ghost events to us.

But is a ghost history, a spectral history, still a history?

Not only have we lost utopia as an ideal end, but historical time itself is also lost, in its continuity and its unfolding. Something like a short-circuit has occurred, a switch shift of the temporal dimension—effects preceding causes, ends preceding origins—and these have led to the paradox of achieved utopia. Now, achieved utopia puts paid to the utopian dimension. It creates an impossible situation, in the sense that it exhausts the possibilities. From this point on, the goal is no longer life transformed, which was the maximal utopia, but rather life-as-survival, which is a kind of minimal utopia.

So today, with the loss of utopias and ideologies, we lack objects of belief. But even worse, perhaps, we lack *objects in which not to believe*. For it is vital—maybe even more vital—to have things in which not to believe. Ironic objects, so to speak, dis-invested practices, ideas to believe or disbelieve as you like. Ideologies performed this ambiguous function pretty well. All this is now jeopardized, vanishing progressively into extreme reality and extreme operationality.

Other things are emerging: retrospective utopias, the revival of all earlier or archaic forms of what is, in a sense, a retrospective or necrospective history. For the disappearance of avant-gardes, those emblems of modernity, has not brought the disappearance of the rearguard as well. Just the opposite is true. In this process of general retroversion (was history perhaps infected with a retrovirus?), the rearguard finds itself in point position.

Quite familiar by now is the parodic, palinodic event, the event Marx analyzed when he depicted Napoleon III as a grotesque copy of Napoleon I. In this second event—a cheap avatar of the original—we have a form of dilution, of historical entropy: history self-repeating becomes farce. The fake history presents itself as if it were advancing and continuing, when it is actually collapsing. The current period offers numerous examples of this debased, extenuated form of the primary events of modernity. Ghost-events, clone-events, *faux*-events, phantom-events—such as phantom limbs, those missing legs or arms that hurt even when they are no longer there. Spectrality, of communism in particular.

Events that are more or less ephemeral because they no longer have any resolution except in the media (where they have the "resolution" images do, where they are "resolved" in high definition)—they have no political resolution. We have a history that no longer consists of action, of acts, but instead culminates in a virtual acting-out; it retains a spectral air of déja-vu. Sarajevo is a fine example of this unreal history, in which all the participants were just standing by, unable to act. It is no longer an event, but rather the symbol of a specific impotence of history. Everywhere, virtuality—the media hyperspace and the hyperspace of discourses—develops in a way diametrically opposed to what one might call, if it still existed, the real movement of history.

——

In the past the virtual was intended to become actual: actuality was its destination. Today the function of the virtual is to proscribe the actual. Virtual history is here in place of real history; the information-replica stands for, stands *in* for, the definitive absence of that real history. Hence our lack of responsibility—both individual and collective—since we are already, by virtue of information, beyond the event, which has not taken place.

We might speak here of a kind of "event strike," to use Macedonio Fernandez's expression. What does this mean? That the work of history is over. That the work of mourning is beginning. That the system of information has been substituted for that of history and is starting to produce events in the same way that Capital is starting to produce Work. Just as labor, under these circumstances, no longer has any significance of its own, the event produced by information has no historical meaning of its own.

This is the point where we enter the transhistorical or transpolitical—that is to say, the sphere where events do not really take place precisely because they are produced and broadcast "in real time," where they have no meaning because they can have all possible meanings. We have, therefore, to grasp them now not politically but transpolitically—that is to say, *at the point where they become lost in the void of information*. The sphere of information is like a space where, after events are deprived of their meaning, they receive an artificial gravity, where, after being flash-frozen politically and historically, they are restaged trans-politically, in real—that is to say, perfectly virtual—time. We might speak in the same way of the transeconomic sphere—in other words, the sphere where classical economics gets lost in the void of speculation, just as History gets lost in the void of information.

But, in the end, perhaps we have to frame all these problems in terms other than the obsolete ones of alienation and the fatal destiny of the subject. And it is precisely the Ubuesque side of this technological outgrowth, of this pro-liferating obscenity and obesity, of this unbridled virtuality, which induces us to do so. Our situation is a wholly pata-physical one—that is to say, everything around us has passed beyond its own limits, has moved beyond the laws of physics and metaphysics. Now, pataphysics is ironic, and the hypothesis that suggests itself here is that, *at the same time that things have reached a state of paroxysm, they have also reached a state of parody.*

Might we advance the hypothesis—beyond the heroic

stage, beyond the critical stage—of an ironic stage of technology, an ironic stage of history, an ironic stage of value? This would at last free us from the Heideggerian vision of technology as the effectuation and final stage of metaphysics; it would free us from all retrospective nostalgia for being, and we would have, instead, a gigantic, objectively ironic vision of the entire scientific and technological process that would not be too far removed from the radical snobbery, the post-historical Japanese snobbery Kojève spoke of.

An ironic reversal of technology, similar to the irony of the media sphere. The common illusion about the media is that they are used by those in power to manipulate, seduce, and alienate the masses. A naive interpretation. The more subtle interpretation, the ironic one, is just the opposite. Through the media, it is the masses who manipulate those in power (or those who believe themselves to be). It is when the political powers think they have the masses where they want them that the masses impose their clandestine strategy of neutralization, of destabilization of a power that has become paraplegic. Finally undecidable; yet both hypotheses are valid, for any interpretation of the media is reversible. It is precisely in this reversibility that the objective irony lies.

Let us put the same hypothesis regarding the object of science—of the most sophisticated of current sciences. Through the most subtle procedures we deploy to capture it, isn't the scientific object itself playing with us, presenting itself as an object and mocking our objective pretension to analyze it? Scientists are not far from admitting this point today, and this irony of the object is the very form of a radical illusion of the world—an illusion no longer physical (illusion of the senses) or metaphysical (illusion of the mind) but pataphysical, in the sense Jarry gave the word when he spoke of pataphysics as "the science of imaginary solutions."

And we can extend the hypothesis to all our technologies, to the technical universe in general. It is becoming the ironic instrument of a world that we only imagine is ours to transform and dominate. It is the world, it is the object itself, that asserts itself, makes itself felt through all the interposing technologies—a process in which we are merely operators. Here again, we see the form of the illusion. Illusion, not error (we are not wrong about technology—there is no human fatality about technology, as is often pretended): the illusion is not an error or deception but a game, a big game whose rules we just don't know and perhaps will never know.

Since the ironic hypothesis—that of a transcendental irony of the technological—is by definition unverifiable, let us take it as undecidable. We are in fact faced with two incompatible hypotheses: that of the perfect crime or, in other words, of the extermination by technology and virtuality of all reality—or that of the ironic game of technology, of an ironic destiny of all science and all knowledge by which the world, and the illusion of the world, are saved and perpetuated. Let us take up both of these irreconcilable and simultaneously "true" perspectives. Nothing allows us to decide between them. "The world is everything which is the case," as Wittgenstein says.

In the *Critique of Political Economy*, Marx writes: "Therefore mankind always sets itself only such tasks as it can solve; since, looking at the matter more closely, it will always be found that the task itself arises only when the material conditions for its solution already exist or are at least in the process of formation." But this no longer holds—precisely because of our world's precipitation into the virtual, which overturns all those "material conditions" Marx was talking about and overturns all those historical conditions that would make it possible to resolve the problems dialectically. The virtual is a form of final solution of history and of all real conflicts. It succeeds so well that today, humanity (or those who would think for humanity) will only set itself problems when they have already been virtually overcome or once the system has successfully displaced and absorbed them. But was this not already the case in the time of Marx? The emergence of the concept of class, and of class struggle, the emergence of the idea of class consciousness marks the moment when class begins progressively to lose its violent, irreducible character. Likewise, if Foucault can analyze power, it is because power no longer has a definition that can be properly called political; it has already become in some sense a lost object. When ethnology turns its attention to primitive societies, it is the sign that they are in the process of disappearing—and what is more, the analyses themselves help to speed their disappearance.

Critical consciousness, thought in general, perhaps, always comes after the fact, a day too late, like Kafka's Messiah—or it comes at the close of the day, like Hegel's owl. It is nothing but retrospective prophecy, or some platonic shadow dancing on the wall of events, in the cavern of history. "If I speak of time," Queneau wrote, "it is because we are already out of time." History doesn't offer a second seating (*L'histoire ne repasse pas les plats*)—only critique does.

Is there space for another kind of thought? An *other* thought—a paradoxical thought that would, in an inversion of the words of Marx, pose only insoluble, definitively insoluble problems? The material conditions for the resolution of such problems are nowhere to be found and never will be found. Is there room for a kind of thought that would instead reproblematize all the old solutions and help to hold the world in enigmatic tension? No one is certain. This may be the risk thought has to take: it must risk falling victim to its own prophecies, just as history risks getting caught in its own snare.

# 3

## THE MURDER OF
## THE REAL

Murder of the Real: it sounds like Nietzsche proclaiming the death of God. But this murder of God was a symbolic one, and it was going to change our destiny. We are still living, metaphysically living off this original crime, as survivors of God. But the Perfect Crime no longer involves God, but Reality, and it is not a symbolic murder but an extermination.

This does not mean what it meant in the Nazi extermination camps. There it was physical and radical. Here it is both more literal and more metaphorical. "*Ex-terminis*": it means that all things (and all beings as well) pass beyond their own end, beyond their own finality, where there is no reality anymore, nor any reason for being, nor any determination (that is why I call it "ex-termination"). Extermination means that nothing is left, no trace, not even a corpse. The corps(e) of the Real—if there is any—has not been recovered, is nowhere to be found. And this because the Real is not just dead (as God is), it has purely and simply disappeared. In our virtual world, the question of the Real, of the referent, of the subject and its object, can no longer even be posed.

I would refer, again, to Elias Canetti, when he writes:

As of a certain point, history was no longer *real*. Without noticing it, all mankind suddenly left reality: everything happening since then was supposedly not true; but we supposedly didn't notice. Our task would now be to find that point, and as long as we didn't have it, we would be forced to abide in our present destruction.

What could be said about this blind point of reversal, where nothing is either true or false any longer and everything is drifting indifferently between cause and effect, between origin and finality? Is it reversible or irreversible? Can we return to the point where the line of history was broken and we were projected to the other side of the mirror? Can we survive the Metastases of the Real as we survived the Death of God? Are we dedicated to survival, or to revival? I would like to give an answer, but promises of the future go the same way as memories of the past: they vanish with the very principle of reality.

For reality is but a concept, or a principle, and by reality I mean the whole system of values connected with this principle. The Real as such implies an origin, an end, a past and a future, a chain of causes and effects, a continuity and a rationality. No real without these elements, without an objective configuration of discourse. And its disappearing is the dislocation of this whole constellation.

Of course, I anticipate a little. In fact, this perfect extermination could only be achieved if the process of virtualization were fully realized. This is not the case, fortunately: as in the best detective novels, the crime is never perfect. Some traces can still be found. We live as if inside Borges's fable of the map and the territory; in this story nothing is left but pieces of the map scattered throughout the empty space of the territory. Except that we must turn the tale upside down: today there is nothing left but a map (the virtual abstraction of the territory), and on this map some fragments of the real are still floating and drifting.

No corpse—no victim either! As for the presumed perpetrator of this Perfect Crime, it's a total mystery: it can be imputed to anyone. No suspect can be identified, not even the weapon—I would say that the weapon used in the crime is the crime itself. Nobody, no class, no group, no subject can be charged with responsibility for this radical actualization of things, of this unconditional hyperrealization of the real. In other words, it is as if all people were murderers and victims simultaneously, reversibly, the two possibilities joined in a kind of Moebius strip. This perverted effect of irresponsibility is a specific aspect of the Perfect Crime. The process itself seems to be irreversible, for it is the very process of rationalization—what we proudly call progress and modernity and liberation—becoming exponential and chaotic.

As for knowing why we go on irreversibly toward this deadline, all we can do is grasp at fantastic hypotheses such as this one: the human species could be dedicating itself to a sort of automatic writing of the world, to an automated and operationalized virtual reality, where human beings as such have no reason for existing anymore. Human subjectivity becomes a set of useless functions, as useless as sexuality is to clones. More generally, all traditional functions—

the critical, the political, the sexual, the social functions—
become useless in a virtual world. Or they survive only in
simulation, like bodybuilding in a disincarnated culture, as
mock functions or alibis. We seem to be driven by a huge
and irresistible compulsion that acts on us through the very
progress of our technologies (expanding for example in
what we call "information highways" and could as well call
"disinformation highways")—a compulsion to draw ever
closer to the unconditional realization of the real.

In virtual reality, absolute transparence converges with
absolute simultaneity. This short circuit and instantaneity
of all things in global information we call "real time." Real
time can be seen as a Perfect Crime perpetrated against time
itself: for with the ubiquity and instant availability of the
totality of information, time reaches its point of perfection,
which is also its vanishing point. Because of course a perfect
time has no memory and no future.

———

Let us be clear about this: if the Real is disappearing, it is not
because of a lack of it—on the contrary, there is too much of

it. It is the excess of reality that puts an end to reality, just as the excess of information puts an end to information, or the excess of communication puts an end to communication. We are no longer dealing with a problematic of lack and alienation, where the referent of the self and the dialectic between subject and object were always to be found, supporting strong and active philosophical positions. The last and most radical analysis of this problematic was achieved by Guy Debord and the Situationists, with their concept of spectacle and spectacular alienation. For Debord there was still a chance of disalienation, a chance for the subject to recover his or her autonomy and sovereignty. But now this radical Situationist critique is over. By shifting to a virtual world, we go beyond alienation, into a state of radical deprivation of the Other, or indeed of any otherness, alterity, or negativity. We move into a world where everything that exists only as idea, dream, fantasy, utopia will be eradicated, because it will immediately be realized, operationalized. Nothing will survive as an idea or a concept. You will not even have time enough to imagine. Events, real events, will not even have time to take place. Everything will be preceded by its virtual realization. We are dealing with an attempt to construct an entirely positive world, a perfect world, expurgated of every illusion, of every sort of evil and negativity, exempt from death itself. This pure, absolute reality, this unconditional realization of the world—this is what I call the Perfect Crime.

This means a crucial mutation from a critical state to a catastrophic one. The real and historical world, with its mass of tensions and contradictions, has always been in crisis. But the state of catastrophe is another thing. It does not mean apocalypse, or annihilation; it means the irruption of something anomalic, which functions according to rules and forms we do not and may never understand. The situation is not simply contradictory or irrational—it is paradoxical. Beyond the end, beyond all finality, we enter a paradoxical state—the state of too much reality, too much positivity, too much information. In this state of paradox, faced with extreme phenomena, we do not know exactly what is taking place.

In any case we cannot trust in traditional values or in the rehabilitation of reality. After all, it may be that humankind, through an enigmatic compulsion, is intimately involved in this catastrophic process and so is doomed to disappear. If this is the case, it would be better by far to treat our disappearance as an art form–to exercise it, to perform it, to create an art of disappearance. Better than the alternative, which would be to vanish without a trace, without even the spectacle of our destruction.

To challenge and to cope with this paradoxical state of things, we need a paradoxical way of thinking; since the world drifts into delirium, we must adopt a delirious point of view. We must no longer assume any principle of truth, of causality, or any discursive norm. Instead, we must grant both the poetic singularity of events and the radical uncertainty of events. It is not easy. We usually think that holding to the protocols of experimentation and verification is the most difficult thing. But in fact the most difficult thing is to renounce the truth and the possibility of verification, to remain as long as possible on the enigmatic, ambivalent, and reversible side of thought.

Truth no longer affords a solution. But perhaps we can aim at a poetic resolution of the world, of the kind promised by history or by language. The actual status of human language today is illuminating. Our common language tries, by discursive means, to inscribe reality in a meaning, in a form of reciprocal exchange. But today language is confronted by the hegemonic fantasy of a global and perpetual communication—the New Order, the new cyberspace of language—where the ultrasimplification of digital languages prevails over the figural complexity of natural languages. With binary coding and decoding the symbolic dimension of language is lost; the materiality, the multiplicity, and the magic of language are erased. At the extreme limit of computation and the coding and cloning of human thought (artificial intelligence), language as a medium of symbolic exchange becomes a definitively useless function. For the first time in history we face the possibility of a Perfect Crime against language, an aphanisis of the symbolic function.

But *a contrario*—the crime is never perfect—we must say that the strongest resistance to this destructive virtualization comes from language itself, from the singularity, the irreducibility, the vernacularity of all languages, which are actually very much alive and which are proving to be the best deterrent against the global extermination of meaning. So the game is not over, but no one can say who will have the last word. More generally speaking, the world and its double cannot occupy the same space, for the double is a perfect artificial and virtual substitute for the world. Conflict between them is inevitable.

———

Now we come to the crucial point. For even as I spoke of the extermination of the Real, I meant, in fact, the more fundamental extermination of the Illusion. But we must be clear about this concept before we go further. I don't mean illusion in the pejorative sense, the negative and irrational concept of illusion as fallacy, fantasmagory, and evil–the illusion whose sole destiny is to be rectified. I mean the radical and objective illusion of the world, the radical impossibility of a real presence of things or beings, their definitive absence from themselves.

For nothing is identical to itself. We are never identical to ourselves, except, perhaps, in sleep and in death. Language itself never signifies what it means; it always signifies something else, through this very irreducible, ontological absence from itself. The probability, in this world, of a total identification, of a total adequation of the same to the same, is equal to zero. Fortunately. For that would be the Perfect Crime—a crime that never happens. In relations between things there is always a hiatus, a distortion, a rift that precludes any reduction of the same to the same. That is even more true for human beings. We are never exactly present to ourselves, or to others. Thus we are not exactly real for one another, nor are we quite real even to ourselves. And this radical alterity is our best chance—our best chance of attracting and being attracted to others, of seducing and being seduced. Put simply, our chance at life.

This concept of radical illusion has analogues in cosmology. Everyone knows that the light of the stars needs a very long time to reach us; sometimes we perceive it after the star itself has disappeared. This gap between the star as a virtual source and its perception by us, this non-simultaneity, is an inescapable part of the illusion of the world, the absence at the heart of the world that constitutes the illusion. And again, this distortion is beneficial. For the simultaneous perception of the light of all the stars would be equivalent to an absolute daylight, and this would be unbearable for us. All the energy of life proceeds from this vital alternation of day and night, and more generally, from this vital mediation. Illusion is the general rule of the universe; reality is but an exception. If the same were identical to the same, we would be faced with an absolute reality, with the unconditional truth of things. But absolute truth is the other name for death. Fortunately, I do not know of any theory or intellectual construction that could–with its commitment to "unconditional truth"–destroy this fantastic material and vital illusion.

We can also find traces of the illusion in the history of the formation of the universe after the Big Bang. The moment it happened, a gigantic cooling-off began; as a result, the universe came into being with the generation of matter and antimatter. Very soon after that, matter separated off from antimatter and gradually evolved into the universe with which we are familiar. Thus the materiality of the world is a restricted one, expurgated of antimatter. Which, volatilized, forms a kind of invisible parallel world, an anti-universe, about which we know almost nothing but on which astrophysics is focusing a great deal of attention. Illusion, or the Mirror of Illusion, is an appropriate name for this invisible, powerful antisubstance, whose interaction with our world would mean an annihilation of matter in the production of pure light. Reality would be obliterated in the clash, matter lost in the chasm with its counterpart . . . .

What is striking about this is that our reality, our "objective" reality, is the result of the amputation of antimatter. This restricted and limited form of matter is what we call reality. I find it at least on the symbolic level both enigmatic and ironic that our reality, born of a radical simplification of the cosmos, has no truth value anymore–divested of its counterpart, its dark half, our world is a definitive illusion.

That this our real world, this restricted materiality, obeys precise physical laws, is not enough to make it true, since this relative coherence is only the paradoxical consequence of this "ontological" simplification. Besides, this matter without antimatter becomes the field of the whole process of entropy and involution, according to the Second Law of Thermodynamics. Because of this rupture of symmetry, the destiny of matter, denuded of antimatter, is attrition. Our task, today, is to delocalize these hypotheses about the universe and to redeploy them at a higher level, where they might challenge our principles of reality and relationality.

Of course, I am well aware that all this is metaphorical. But we are not interested in generating one more truth. We are trying to recover the traces of the illusion, that is to say, the vestiges of the original crime against negativity that started with the elimination of antimatter. Against the extermination of evil, of death, of illusion, against this Perfect Crime, we must fight for the criminal imperfection of the world. Against this artificial paradise of technicity and virtuality, against the attempt to build a world completely positive, rational, and true, we must save the traces of the illusory world's definitive opacity and mystery.

But are we ready to play the paradoxical, catastrophic, and ironic game that this radical illusion seems to propose? It would mean a drastic revision not only of the principle of reality but also of the principle of knowledge. "Knowledge" normally implies a dialectic between subject and object, a field of representation where the subject is master of the

game, since the subject constructed the frame of representation and projected it into the world. This presupposes the
privilege of the subject and the concomitant inferior status
of the object, including the scientific object. But knowledge
rules over truth and causal relations, not over appearance
or illusion. In the domain of the illusion, knowledge is no
longer logically possible, for its principles and postulates
cannot function. And this is not just a metaphysical insight:
today the microsciences stand at the point where the object
as such no longer exists. It vanishes, it escapes, it has no def-
inite status, it only appears in the form of ephemeral and
aleatory traces on the screens of virtualization. At their
outer edge the most advanced sciences can only verify the
object's disappearance. In other words, they can only verify
the way the object plays with its own objectivity. This is the
object's perverse strategy; perhaps it is a form of revenge.
Apparently, the object is a trickster, foiling all the protocols
of the subject's experiment, so that the subject itself loses its
position as subject.

Science has got it wrong. It is true that, thanks to the
progress of analsyis and technique, we actually discover the

world in all its complexity—its atoms, particles, molecules, viruses. But never has science postulated, even as science fiction, that things discover us at the same time that we discover them, according to an inexorable reversibility. We always thought that things were passively waiting to be discovered, in much the same way that America is imagined to have been waiting for Columbus. But it is not so. At the moment when the subject discovers the object—whether it is an "Indian" or a virus—the object makes a reversible, but never innocent, discovery of the subject. More—it is actually a sort of invention of the subject by the invented object.

Knowledge, defined conventionally, always proceeds in the same direction, from the subject to the object. But today processes of reversion are emerging everywhere—in areas from anthropology to viral pathology. It is as if we had torn the object from its opaque and inoffensive stillness, from its indifference, from the deep secret where it was asleep. Today the object wakes up and reacts, determined to keep its secret alive. This duel engaged in by the subject and the object means the loss of the subject's hegemonic position: the object becomes the horizon of the subject's disappearance. Obviously, this new scenario, this new dramaturgy, is opposed to the classic theory of knowledge.

In this light, reality itself becomes problematic. Like an obsequious servant, it obeys any hypothesis, verifying them all in turn, even when they contradict each other. Reality does not care about the knowledge we are distilling from our observation and analysis of its behavior. Indifferent to every truth, reality becomes a sort of sphinx, enigmatic in its hyperconformity, simulating itself as virtuality or reality show. Reality becomes hyperreality–paroxysm and parody all at once. It supports all sorts of interpretations because it no longer makes sense, because it no longer wants to be interpreted. But this unintelligibility is not mystical or romantic: it is ironic. Irony is the last sign that comes from the secret core of the object, the modern allegory of the reversibility of all things.

Here again, it is not the question of a subjective, critical irony but of an objective irony linked to the radical material illusion of the world and its unexpected effects. Things have become so accelerated that processes are no longer inscribed in a linear temporality, in a linear unfolding of history. Nothing moves any longer from cause to effect: everything is transversalized by inversions of meaning, by perverse events, by ironic reversals. Acceleration, streams and turbulences, self-potentialization and chaotic effects. And this deregulation of the system is actually the work of the system itself (just as Marx said of the proletariat, that its emancipation would be the work of the proletarians themselves: ironically, the formula also applies to the self-annihilating system). Pushed to extremes of sophistication and performance, to a point of perfection and totalization (as is the virtual system of nets and information), the system reaches its breaking point and implodes all by itself. This does not occur through the actions of any critical subject or any historical forces of subversion: it occurs through ultra-realization and automatic reversal, pure and simple.

This is what I call objective irony: there is a strong probability, verging on a certainty, that systems will be undone by their own systematicity. This is true not only for technical structures but for human ones as well. The more these political, social, economic systems advance toward their own perfection, the more they deconstruct themselves. This is very clear in the field of media and multimedia, where, because of an excess of information, we have lost access to real information and real historical events. But this logic is at work in religious, sexual, and productive fields as well. And even at a scientific level: the more the object is persecuted by experimental procedures, the more it invents strategies of counterfeit, evasion, disguise, disappearance. It is like a virus; it escapes by endlessly inventing counterstrategies. This behavior of the object is also ironic insofar as it breaks the foolish pretensions of the subject, its desire to impose laws and dispose of the world according to its own will, its own representations. Today the world itself engages in dissidence, disobeying, in its paradoxicality, even the laws of physics (very different from the human transgression of human laws, which lacks the irony implicit in the dissidence of the object).

I won't transform the object into a supersubject. But it would seem that something has escaped us. Definitively. This is not because our science and technologies are not advanced enough; on the contrary. The closer we come, through experimentation, to the object, the more it steals away from us and finally becomes undecidable. And do not ask where it has gone. Simply, the object is *what escapes the subject*—more we cannot say, since our position is still that of the subject and of rational discourse. At any rate, we cannot rely on the pretext of an insufficient development of the scientific, intellectual or mental apparatus. The apparatus has given all that it can give; it has even passed beyond its own definitions of rationality. I cannot tell you exactly, in seconds, the decimal point of Planck's constant beyond which there will be no further possible knowledge of the cosmos, because light does not exist, and accurate representation is impossible. It is the event horizon, as they say in physics, beyond which nothing makes sense and nothing at all may be discovered.

That, if there is any, is the secret of the universe. As a metaphor, I would say that at the core of every human being and every thing there is such a fundamentally inaccessible secret. That is the vital illusion of which Nietzsche spoke, the glass wall of truth and illusion. From our rational point of view, this may appear rather desperate and could even justify something like pessimism. But from the point of view of singularity, of alterity, of secret and seduction, it is, on the contrary, our only chance: our last chance. In this sense, the Perfect Crime is an hypothesis of radiant optimism.

Of course, it is a matter of tragic optimism, as it is expressed in the famous line of Hölderlin: "But where danger is, grows the saving power also" (*Wo die Gefahr wächst, wächst das Rettende auch*). It applies today—with the caveat that, as the evil genius of modernity has changed our destiny, Hölderlin's phrase must be reversed: the more the saving power grows, the greater the danger. For we are no longer victims of an excess of fate and danger, of illusion and death. We are victims of an absence of destiny, of a lack of illusion, and consequently of an excess of reality, security, and efficiency. What hangs over us is the excess of protection and positivity—the unconditional "saving" performed by our technologies. But it seems that something resists this irresistible trend, something irreducible. And here we might quote, as a counterpart to Hölderlin's phrase, this very mysterious sentence by Heidegger: "When we look into the ambiguous essence of technology, we behold the constellation, the stellar course of the mystery."

This sentence is quite enigmatic, since it seems to contradict Heidegger's interpretation of technology as "negative ontology," as a loss of being, as a definitive unveiling of the secret of the universe, as a disenchanted inspection, an *"arraisonnement"* (*Gestell*) of the world, in short, as the Perfect Crime itself. The alternative would be that, at the extreme horizon of technology, something else happens, another game, with other rules. The point is that the constellation of the secret still resists, remains alive. Either we think of technology as the exterminator of Being, the exterminator of the secret, of seduction and appearances, or we imagine that technology, by way of an ironic reversibility, might be an immense detour toward the radical illusion of the world. A massive "clinamen," a hidden strategy moving behind all our techniques and practices, an absolutely unpredictable movement that would finally bring us to the other side of metaphysics. We might then, through this detour, break through the mirror of technology–*contra* Heidegger, for whom technology is still the absolute achievement of metaphysics. Technology as delusion, technology as definitive illusion.

But we cannot be certain about this virtual end of things. There is no way to choose between these alternative hypotheses, and we must be aware that at the end of all possible theory, we shall have to deal with two antinomic eventualities–and that this fatal situation will never be resolved.

Here, however, lies the task of any philosophical thought: to go to the limit of hypotheses and processes, even if they are catastrophic. The only justification for thinking and writing is that it accelerates these terminal processes. Here, beyond the discourse of truth, resides the poetic and enigmatic value of thinking. For, facing a world that is unintelligible and problematic, our task is clear: we must make that world even more unintelligible, even more enigmatic.

# NOTES

## 1. THE FINAL SOLUTION

*p. 4: "These, then, are the experimental and artificial forms of cloning–not including Dolly, of course, and the rest of her kind."* Perhaps the most famous sheep in history, Dolly is the first mammal to have been successfully cloned from adult cells. The cloning was performed by Ian Wilmut and his colleagues at the Roslin Institute, Edinburgh, Scotland, in March 1997.

*p. 5: "on board the US satellite Discoverer 17." The Discoverer 17* was launched into the earth's orbit November 12, 1960.

*p. 16: "Such was the lesson of Biosphere 2, the artificial synthesis of all the planet's systems, the ideal copy of the human race and its environment."* Biosphere 2 is an experimental microcosm, a sealed glass and metal structure approximately 204,000 cubic meters in size, located in the Santa Catalina Mountains of Arizona. It contains seven different "ecosystems," which include an ocean (housed in a vast stainless steel container), a savanna, and a rain forest, and is the site of ongoing research into such topics as the effect of rising concentrations of $CO_2$ on coral reefs. Biosphere 2 is currently affiliated with Columbia University.

*pp. 18–19: "It is as if, through this self-inflicted violence, humanity wants to make itself ready from now on to be the survivor of some great impending catastrophe."* Elias Canetti may be able to help us understand Baudrillard's antipathy for the survivor. In *Crowds and Power*, trans. Carol Stewart (New York: The Noonday Press, Farrar, Straus and Giroux, 1984); originally published as *Masse und Macht* (Hamburg: Claasen Verlag, 1960), Canetti analyzes the often megalomanic drive for power that he discerns in the survivor:

> All man's designs on immortality contain something of this desire for survival. He does not only want to exist for always, but to exist when others are no longer there. He wants to live longer than everyone else, and to *know* it; and when he is no longer there himself, his name must continue (pp. 227).

*p. 24: "(une pensée unique)"* After some hesitation, I decided to coin the term "monothought" in an attempt to emphasize the elements of normativity and univocality that I perceived in Baudrillard's *une pensée unique*. "Monothought" hints at aspects of our cultural conditioning that render us interchangeable. It is meant to evoke a parallel with monocrop agriculture, an aggressive, intensive use of agricultural land; it can be deployed on a very large scale and produce high yields, but it has serious long-term consequences. Monothought, not unlike monocrop agriculture, lays waste to the very human cultural structures that it seeks to make more streamlined and "efficient."

# 1. THE FINAL SOLUTION

*p. 24: "*We *invented the distinction, and* we *are in the process of erasing it."* Baudrillard's "we," here, should perhaps be read as "we the legatees of Enlightenment thought," rather than exclusively as "we Westerners" or "we Anglo-Europeans."

# 2. THE MILLENNIUM, OR THE SUSPENSE OF THE YEAR 2000

*p. 34: "This is why I advanced the idea that the Year 2000 would not take place. . . ."* The lecture was delivered on May 27, 1999, and in its original form it was an artifact of its time, balanced on the leading edge of the millennium, pointing "ahead" to a nonevent which we, of course, did not experience. Some of the tenses have been altered to reflect our new position vis-à-vis the end, but many of them have been left as they were written, in a "suspended" present.

*p. 37: "When there is overall transparence, when everything can be seen, nothing can be* foreseen *anymore."* "Transparence" is Baudrillard translator Chris Turner's rendering of the French *"transparence,"* and is meant to help distinguish the term from everyday "transparency."

*p. 38: "The countdown is the code of the automatic disappearance of the world, and all our little charitable machines, by way of which we anticipate that disappearance—the telethons, Sidathons, and all kinds of Thanathons—are merely the promotional sales events for the misery of this fin de siècle."* "SIDA" is the French acronym for Acquired Immune System Deficiency; a "Sidathon" is a benefit held to raise money for the victims of AIDS (see, for example, the 1997 Sidathon organized by the group Sid'Afrique to benefit AIDS victims on the Ivory Coast).

*p. 41: "As a result, the ozone layer that was protecting memory becomes frayed; the hole through which memories and time are leaking out into space expands, prefiguring the great migration of the void to the periphery."* This is an allusion to Alfred Jarry's inversion of the law of falling bodies: "Contemporary science is founded upon the principle of induction: most people have seen a certain phenomenon precede or follow some other phenomenon most often, and conclude therefrom that it will ever be thus. . . .

Instead of formulating the law of the fall of a body toward a center, how far more apposite would be the law of the ascension of a vacuum toward a periphery, a vacuum being considered a unit of non-density, a hypothesis far less arbitrary than the choice of a concrete unit of positive density such as *water*?" (*Selected Works of Alfred Jarry*, ed. Roger Shattuck and Simon Watson Taylor [New York: Grove Press, 1965], p. 193).

*p. 42: "The concept of countdown evokes once again Arthur C. Clarke's 'The Nine Billion Names of God' "* In Arthur C. Clarke, *The Nine Billion Names of God* (New York: Harcourt Brace World, 1967).

*p. 45: "Obesity and obscenity form the contrapuntal figure for all our systems, which have been seized by something of an Ubuesque distension."* Baudrillard here and elsewhere is alluding to Alfred Jarry's notorious invention Père Ubu, around whom Jarry wrote several satirical, highly scatalogical plays and vignettes. Depicted as monstrously obese, Ubu wreaks havoc everywhere he goes (in Ubu's earliest appearance, Jarry has him flush his conscience down the toilet). Of Ubu, Roger Shattuck writes:

"We are all Ubu, still blissfully ignorant of our destructive-ness and systematically practicing the soul-devouring 'reversal' of flushing our conscience down the john. Ubu, unruffled king of tyrants and cuckolds, is more terrifying than tragedy" ("Introduction," in *Selected Works of Alfred Jarry*, ed. Roger Shattuck and Simon Watson Taylor [New York: Grove Press, 1965], p. 10).

*p. 51: We might speak here of a kind of "event strike," to use Macedonio Fernandez's expression.* The Argentine writer and metaphysician Macedonio Fernandez (1874-1952). His works strongly influenced Jorge Luis Borges, and are today considered to be important precursors of the con-temporary Latin American novel. Macedonio's concept of the event strike can be found in his *Papeles de Recien-venido. Continuación de la nada* (Buenos Aires: Editorial Losada, S.A., 1944).

*p. 53: "We would have, instead, a gigantic, objectively ironic vision of the entire scientific and technological process that would not be too far removed from the radi-cal snobbery, the post-historical Japanese snobbery Kojève spoke of."* This reference can be found in Alexandre

## 2. THE MILLENNIUM

Kojève's "Note to the Second Edition" in "Interpretation of the Third Part of Chapter VIII of *Phenomenology of Spirit*" in *Introduction to the Reading of Hegel* (Ed. Allan Bloom, trans. James H. Nichols, Jr. [New York: Basic 1969] [orig. publ. as *Introduction à la lecture de Hegel* (2nd ed. Paris: Gallimard, 1947)], pp. 159–162). In this note, the "natural" post-historical society of America is (unfavorably) compared with what Kojève calls the "snobbism" of post-historical Japan. For Kojève, Japanese "snobbism"–the production of purely arbitrary social and cultural forms, of an artifical, "empty" symbolic ordering of human society–is a compelling alternative approach to the problem of the end of history (and the concomitant loss of tensions, of "necessary" cultural forms, implicit in that ending). This "snobbism," by virtue of its very emptiness, has striking affinities with the arbitrary creativity of the pataphysical response to a "world without limits" that for Baudrillard would characterize an ironic stage of history.

*p. 54: "Scientists are not far from admitting this point today, and this irony of the object is the very form of a radical illusion of the world–an illusion no longer physical (illusion of the senses) or metaphysical (illusion of the mind) but pataphysical, in the sense Jarry gave the word when he spoke of pataphysics as 'the science of imaginary solutions.'* " This phrase can be found in Roger Shattuck's "Superliminal Note" on pataphysics, published originally in *Evergreen Review* 4, no. 2 (May–June 1960); the line was also used by the Collège de Pataphysique in their pamphlet, "On the Threshhold of 'Pataphysics" (Paris: "XC," 1963?).

*p. 55: "Nothing allows us to decide between them. 'The world is everything which is the case,' as Wittgenstein says."Tractatus Logico-Philosophicus,* trans. D. F. Pears and B. F. McGuinness (London: Routledge & Kegan Paul, 1961), 1:7; orig. publ. as *Logisch-philosophische Abhandlung* in *Annalen der Naturphilosophie,* ed. Wilhelm Ostwald, 1921.

*pp. 55–56: "In the* Critique of Political Economy, *Marx writes: 'Therefore mankind always sets itself only such tasks as it can solve; since, looking at the matter more closely, it will always be found that the task itself arises only when the material conditions for its solution already exist or are at least in the process of formation.'* " In Karl

Marx and Frederick Engels, *Selected Works*, vol. 2 (Moscow: Lawrence and Wishart, 1935), pp. 361 ff.

   *p. 57:* " *'If I speak of time,'* Queneau wrote, *'it is because we are already out of time.'* " Baudrillard is probably quoting a line from Raymond Queneau's poem, "L'Explication des métaphores," in the collection *Les Ziaux*: "Si je parle d'un lieu, c'est qu'il a disparu / Si je parle du temps, c'est qu'il n'est déjà plus" (*Les Ziaux*: Paris, Gallimard, Métamorphoses, 1948).

## 3. THE MURDER OF THE REAL

   *p. 61: "the Perfect Crime"* This concept is drawn from Baudrillard's earlier book *The Perfect Crime* (trans. Chris Turner. London, New York: Verso, 1996 [orig. publ. as *Le crime parfait*, Paris, Editions Galilée, 1995]). In this book Baudrillard lays out the disastrous consequences of the expurgation of otherness, absence, and negativity from contemporary Western culture, a "crime" that would efface not only its victim but also all evidence that the crime took place.

## 3. THE MURDER OF THE REAL

*p. 62: "I would refer, again, to Elias Canetti, when he writes:*

As of a certain point, history was no longer real. Without noticing it, all mankind suddenly left reality: everything happening since then was supposedly not true; but we supposedly didn't notice. Our task would now be to find that point, and as long as we didn't have it, we would be forced to abide in our present destruction."

Elias Canetti, *The Human Province*, trans. Joachim Neugroschel (New York: Seabury Press, 1978), p. 69.

*p. 69: "For the first time in history we face the possibility of a Perfect Crime against language, an aphanisis of the symbolic function."* This term may well be drawn from psychoanalytic parlance. Based upon the Greek for "disappearing" or "fading," "aphanisis" was a term initially developed by Ernest Jones to describe a fear of the loss or waning of desire, a fear that Jones identified in both sexes and perceived to be more fundamental than the castration complex. Lacan also uses the term, although it acquires a different resonance in his work, where it is used to discuss the "fading" or disappearance of the subject as it is in the process of being constituted in and by language, the loss engendered by the constellation of the subject as split by language. See, for example, Lacan's *The Four Fundamental Concepts of Psychoanalysis* (ed. Jacques-Alain Miller, trans. Alan Sheridan [New York: Norton, 1981]); orig. publ. as *Le Seminaire de Jacques Lacan, Livre XI: "Les quatre concepts fondamentaux de la psychanalyse"* [Editions du Seuil, 1973], pp. 217ff). To argue, as Baudrillard does, that the symbolic function itself may be doomed to disappear, implies the loss of the "loss" that this symbolic function instantiates in the subject as delineated by Lacan. There is no communication possible under these terms; there is only code. (Thanks to Professor Norah Ashe.)

*p. 81: "And here we might quote, as a counterpart to Hölderlin's phrase, this very mysterious sentence by Heidegger: 'When we look into the ambiguous essence of technology, we behold the constellation, the stellar course of the mystery.'"* Martin Heidegger, *The Question Concerning Technology and Other Essays*, trans. William Lovitt (New York: Harper and Row, 1977), p. 33.

# INDEX